SCHOLASTIC

Let's Find Out™

Let's Talk About Opposites,
Morning to Night

Laine Falk · Joan Michael

Children's Press®
A Division of Scholastic Inc.
New York Toronto London Auckland Sydney
Mexico City New Delhi Hong Kong
Danbury, Connecticut

Literacy Specialist: Francie Alexander, Chief Academic Officer, Scholastic Inc.
Art Director: Joan Michael

Photographs: James Levin (girl); ©David Young-Wolff/Getty Images (bus)
Illustrations: Eric Larsen

Library of Congress Cataloging-in-Publication Data

Falk, Laine, 1974-
  Let's talk about opposites, morning to night / written by Laine Falk.
    p. cm. — (Let's find out)
  ISBN-13: 978-0-531-14872-3 (lib. bdg.)
  ISBN-10: 0-531-14872-6 (lib. bdg.)
  1. English language—Synonyms and antonyms—Juvenile literature. I.
Title. II. Series.

PE1591.F248 2007
428.1—dc22   2006026328

1 2 3 4 5 6 7 8 9 10 R 16 15 14 13 12 11 10 09 08 07

I had a great day yesterday!
Let me tell you about everything I did.

I woke up hungry. I had my favorite breakfast. My plate was **full**.

I ate everything!
My plate was empty.

Time for school! I rode the bus. There's a big hill on the way. We went **over** it.

There's a bridge on the way too!
We went **under** it.

At recess, I played outside with my friends.
We were **loud**!

At reading time, we read our favorite books.
We were quiet.

It was my turn to feed our class pet.
I put a carrot into the open cage.

I watched him eat when the cage was closed. He loves carrots!

Next, we got ready to draw pictures.
All my crayons were **in** their box.

I took them **OUT** of the box.
Using lots of colors is fun!

Soon it was time to go home.
We lined up for the bus.
I was at the front of the line.

My friend Jake was at the **back** of the line.

After school, I took my dog

for a walk. We went to the top **of the hill.**

I looked down and saw Jake!
He was at the bottom of the hill.

For dinner, we ate yummy soup.
It was **hot!** We had to blow on it.

For dessert, we had frozen fruit pops.
They were cold.

After I ate, my face was dirty!

But I always wash up before bed. I made sure my face was **clean**.

At bedtime, I was still wide awake.
So I read a book.

But soon I felt very tired.
I fell fast asleep!

Can you find these opposites?
Go back and look at the pictures in this book.

 This towel is clean. Can you find the dirty towel?

 This dog is going under the fence.
Can you find the dog jumping over the fence?

 This window is closed.
Can you find the open window?

 This bird is loud. Can you find the quiet bird?

 This glass is full. Can you find the empty glass?

 These blocks are out of the box.
Can you find the blocks that are in the box?

 This bear is awake.
Can you find the bear that is asleep?

What other opposites can you find?

Look for